FEDERAL FORCES

CAREERS AS FEDERAL AGENTS

A CAREER AS AN FBI SPECIAL AGENT

Daniel R. Faust

PowerKiDS press

New York

Published in 2016 by The Rosen Publishing Group, Inc.
29 East 21st Street, New York, NY 10010

First Edition

Editor: Caitlin McAneney
Book Design: Mickey Harmon

Photo Credits: Cover (woman) Digital Vision/Thinkstock.com; cover (background) Digital Storm/Shutterstock.com; cover (logo) Color Symphony/Shutterstock.com; cover, pp. 1, 3–32 (mesh texture) Eky Studio/Shutterstock.com; p. 5 (wood grain) restyler/Shutterstock.com; p. 5 (emblem) Chip Somodevilla/Getty Images News/Getty Images; p. 7 FPG/Staff/Archive Photos/Getty Images; p. 9 (Bonnie and Clyde) https://en.wikipedia.org/wiki/Bonnie_and_Clyde#/media/File:Bonnieclyde_f.jpg; p. 9 (John F. Kennedy) https://en.wikipedia.org/wiki/John_F._Kennedy#/media/File:John_F._Kennedy,_White_House_color_photo_portrait.jpg; p. 11 (main) Leah-Anne Thompson/Shutterstock.com; p. 11 (J. Edgar Hoover) https://en.wikipedia.org/wiki/J._Edgar_Hoover#/media/File:HooverJEdgar-LOC.jpg; p. 13 Miami Herald/Contributor/Tribune News Service/Getty Images; p. 14 DmitriMaruta/Shutterstock.com; p. 15 https://en.wikipedia.org/wiki/File:FBI_Badge_%26_gun.jpg; p. 17 Remi BENALI/Contributor/Gamma-Rapho/Getty Images; p. 19 Courtesy of the Federal Bureau of Investigation; p. 21 Courtesy of the United States Army; p. 23 Patrick AVENTURIER/Contributor/Gamma-Rapho/Getty Images; p. 25 (main) Mark Van Scyoc/Shutterstock.com; p. 25 (inset) Anthony Correia/Shutterstock.com; p. 27 Michael Bocchieri/Staff/Getty Images News/Getty Images; p. 29 John Moore/Staff/Getty Images News/Getty Images; p. 30 Artamonov Yury/Shutterstock.com.

Cataloging-in-Publication Data

Faust, Daniel R.
A career as an FBI special agent / by Daniel R. Faust.
p. cm. — (Federal forces: careers as federal agents)
Includes index.
ISBN 978-1-4994-1060-0 (pbk.)
ISBN 978-1-4994-1096-9 (6 pack)
ISBN 978-1-4994-1115-7 (library binding)
1. United States. — Federal Bureau of Investigation — Vocational guidance — Juvenile literature. 2. United States. — Federal Bureau of Investigation — Officials and employees — Juvenile literature. I. Faust, Daniel R. II. Title.
HV8144.F43 F38 2016
363.25023'73—d23

Manufactured in the United States of America

CPSIA Compliance Information: Batch #WS15PK: For Further Information contact Rosen Publishing, New York, New York at 1-800-237-9932

Contents

What's the FBI?

The FBI, which stands for the Federal Bureau of Investigation, is the main investigative agency of the U.S. Department of Justice. Its mission includes defending the United States from **terrorists** and foreign threats, enforcing the criminal laws of the United States, and providing assistance to federal, state, local, and foreign agencies.

The FBI has the widest authority of all federal law enforcement agencies. The FBI investigates cases involving national—or domestic—and international terrorism, **corruption**, drugs, organized crime, civil rights violations, and violent crime. The FBI works closely with local, national, and international agencies as part of joint **task forces**. Read on to learn more about the FBI and how you can land a career with this important federal agency.

The symbols on the FBI seal represent justice, unity, strength, and peace. The FBI motto—"Fidelity, Bravery, Integrity"—best describes the qualities of the men and women who work for the agency.

The History of the FBI

As early as the 1880s, the U.S. government was aware of the need for a national law enforcement agency to help identify and watch criminals. Many citizens were afraid the government would use such an agency as a secret police force. However, both President Theodore Roosevelt and Attorney General Charles Bonaparte knew it was necessary.

On July 26, 1908, Bonaparte created the Bureau of Investigation—a 34-person investigative agency that reported to the U.S. Department of Justice. In 1932, it was renamed the United States Bureau of Investigation. One year later, the agency was linked to the Bureau of **Prohibition** and renamed the Division of Investigation. In 1935, the agency was renamed the Federal Bureau of Investigation and became an independent agency within the Department of Justice.

The FBI and Great Depression Criminals

The Great Depression was an economic downturn in world history that lasted from 1929 through the 1930s. Many Americans became very poor, and some turned to a life of serious crime. Bonnie Parker and Clyde Barrow were a couple that robbed and murdered people across several states from 1932 to 1934. The FBI finally tracked them down on May 23, 1934, and killed them. George Kelly, called Machine Gun Kelly, and his gang of criminals kidnapped a rich oil businessman. The FBI caught Kelly and his wife on September 26, 1933.

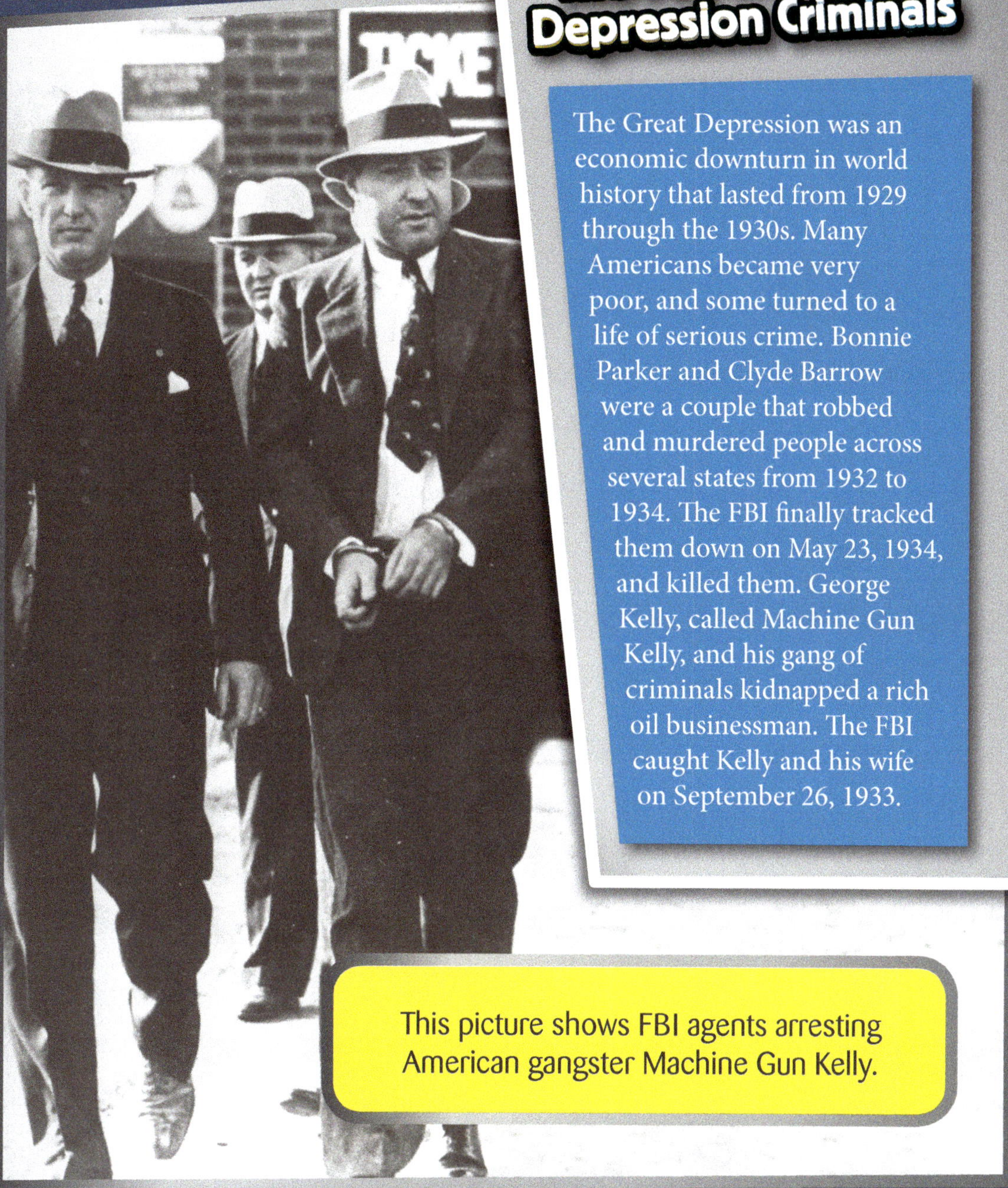

This picture shows FBI agents arresting American gangster Machine Gun Kelly.

Catching Criminals

According to its official mission, the FBI's goal is "to protect and defend the United States against terrorist and foreign intelligence threats and to enforce the criminal laws of the United States." To accomplish this goal, the FBI has **jurisdiction** to investigate more than 200 categories, or classes, of federal law.

You're probably most familiar with the FBI from movies and television shows. The agency is often portrayed by Hollywood as chasing bank robbers, serial killers, or members of organized crime. While they do investigate these kinds of crimes, FBI agents investigate other kinds of crime, too. During Prohibition, the FBI investigated bootleggers, or people who made, transported, and sold alcohol illegally. Today, the FBI investigates hate crimes, gangs, identity theft, kidnapping, cyber (Internet) crimes, and crimes against children.

Famous FBI Cases

1929 – 1931
Al Capone's organized crime ring

1932 – 1934
Bonnie and Clyde's crime spree

1950
Julius and Ethel Rosenberg spy case

1963
John F. Kennedy assassination

1963 – 1977
Sixteenth Street Baptist Church bombing

1971 – present
D.B. Cooper's plane hijacking

1978 – 1996
The Unabomber's mailed bombs

1985 – 1992
John Gotti's organized crime reign

1995
Oklahoma City bombing

2011
9/11 terrorist attacks

Bonnie and Clyde

John F. Kennedy

The FBI has been around for over 100 years. In that time, it's participated in the investigation of countless famous crimes.

Different Jobs at the FBI

With about 35,000 employees around the world, the FBI has many different kinds of jobs. Not everyone who works for the FBI is a special agent. The FBI employs people from a wide range of professional fields.

One of the FBI's missions is to collect and share intelligence, or secret information about one's enemies, with other law enforcement agencies around the world. The FBI relies on intelligence specialists to collect, **analyze**, and report important information. The FBI also employs men and women with science and technology backgrounds, including engineering, mathematics, and **forensics**. The FBI works around the world, so it needs employees who can speak, read, and write in multiple foreign languages. The agency also employs people who specialize in business, finance, design, and even flying planes.

J. Edgar Hoover

John Edgar Hoover was born on January 1, 1895, in Washington, D.C. After graduating from high school, he started working for the Library of Congress and went to law school. In 1924, Hoover was named director of the agency that would one day be called the FBI. He instituted many changes, particularly regarding the qualifications required to become special agents. Hoover served as director of the FBI until 1972. Under his leadership, the agency became an important part of the national government.

The first FBI special agents were expected to have a degree in accounting or criminal law. Today, the FBI relies on people from a wide variety of backgrounds, such as engineering or science.

What Is a Special Agent?

In the United States, a special agent is an investigator working for a federal, state, or local government. Special agents conduct criminal investigations and have the authority to make arrests. Although the FBI is not the only law enforcement agency in the United States that has special agents, FBI special agents are probably the most well-known.

Because the FBI is responsible for enforcing different kinds of laws, the career of an FBI special agent can follow several different paths. Special agents assigned to the counterterrorism division gather and analyze information in order to identify terrorist threats. Criminal investigation agents examine cases of financial crime, civil rights offenses, organized crime, and corruption. Counterintelligence agents identify foreign threats to national security, and intelligence agents examine information that can be critical to investigations.

Cyber agents use their knowledge of computer technology to combat the growing threat of cyber crime. As technology improves, the FBI continues to hire and train computer experts.

Working in the Field

Each day as an FBI special agent is filled with new jobs and challenges. Because the FBI fills many different positions in the law enforcement community, special agents must perform a wide variety of duties each day.

Some days, a special agent may be out in the field, gathering evidence, completing searches, or arresting suspects. Other days, an agent may meet with an informant, or source, to gather information about an ongoing investigation. Some special agents also work as lab technicians, in public relations, or as instructors at the FBI Academy.

Of course, like many jobs, a special agent's day is not always filled with danger or excitement. Special agents need to complete paperwork and meet with coworkers, as well as **testify** in federal court.

All FBI special agents are given a badge by the Department of Justice and a sidearm, or weapon, such as a pistol.

Special FBI Teams

Some operations are too difficult or dangerous for a regular special agent. To handle these missions, the FBI created several specialized units. Special FBI teams include the **Hostage** Rescue Team (HRT), Computer Analysis and Response Team (CART), and Special Weapons and Tactics (SWAT) team.

The HRT was formed in 1983 to provide a **tactical** solution for counterterrorism, hostage situations, and other law enforcement operations in the United States and abroad. Qualified and driven special agents volunteer to join the HRT. Members of the HRT receive training in both tactics and equipment. CART is made up of roughly 500 trained special agents and support **personnel**. CART agents analyze computers, cell phones, and digital cameras for information.

SWAT teams are usually the first to respond to cases such as hostage rescues, hijackings, and escaped criminals. Unlike HRT and CART, SWAT positions aren't full-time jobs. Instead, special agents volunteer to go on a SWAT mission when one arises.

Applying for a Job with the FBI

Are you interested in a career as an FBI special agent? Working for the FBI can be a rewarding experience, but it isn't easy. The FBI only hires the most commited and qualified individuals.

Because the FBI is responsible for investigating different kinds of crimes, it needs to hire people from different educational backgrounds. Special agents are drawn from the worlds of computer science, criminal justice, finance, engineering, and international relations. All candidates must have excellent verbal and written communication skills, be able to adapt to changing environments, and be driven to achieve their goals. In order to apply for a career with the FBI, you must be a U.S. citizen who's never been proven guilty of a crime, and you must be drug-free.

If you apply for a job as a special agent, be prepared to work hard. FBI training is 20 weeks long and includes both academic, or educational, and physical courses.

Would You Pass the Test?

FBI special agents need to be physically fit. People who apply to the FBI are required to pass a physical fitness test at least three times before and during training. These tests consist of four events: sit-ups, 300-meter sprint, push-ups, and a 1.5-mile (2.4 km) run. If an **applicant** fails the physical fitness test three times, they won't be allowed to continue with their training.

In addition to the physical fitness tests, applicants to the FBI must also meet certain vision and hearing requirements. After all these tests are passed, an applicant must still undergo a full medical review. Applicants must submit their medical records, which are reviewed by the FBI chief medical officer. This officer decides if the applicant has any medical issues or conditions that could prevent them from performing their duties.

Special agents are expected to be in top physical shape at all times. Trainees are given physical fitness tests during their 20 weeks at the FBI Academy.

Life at Quantico

All special agent trainees must attend the FBI Academy in Quantico, Virginia. The FBI Academy, usually just called Quantico, is considered one of the best law enforcement training facilities in the world. Trainees must live on school grounds and follow a stern code of conduct. At Quantico, a trainee's classmates become their family.

A trainee's time at Quantico is divided between classroom and hands-on learning. They're expected to study many different subjects, both investigative and academic. The program includes training in physical fitness, survival skills, defensive tactics, and weapons. A trainee's progress is tested both academically and physically throughout their time at Quantico. When trainees graduate, they take an oath and are officially sworn in as officers.

Inside Hogan's Alley

Hogan's Alley is a realistic training environment built on the grounds of the FBI Academy. Built in 1987, Hogan's Alley resembles a small town complete with homes and businesses, including a hotel and an often-robbed bank. Actors play bad guys and bystanders. Hogan's Alley is where new agents learn the tactics they will need in the real world, including investigation techniques and the use of firearms. In addition to the FBI, other federal, state, and local agencies use Hogan's Alley for training new agents.

Hogan's Alley was built with the help of Hollywood set designers. The realistic training facility covers more than 10 acres (4 ha).

Special Agents Around the World

The current FBI headquarters is located in the J. Edgar Hoover FBI Building in Washington, D.C. FBI headquarters is staffed by officials, special agents, and other professionals who oversee FBI operations around the world. They're responsible for setting FBI policies, serving as a center for intelligence gathering, providing support for agents, and directing operations during national emergencies.

In addition to the national headquarters in Washington, D.C., the FBI has 56 field offices, or divisions, located in major cities across the U.S. and Puerto Rico. These offices investigate local and regional crimes and work closely with local law enforcement agencies on cases and operations. FBI offices called legal attaché offices are responsible for federal law enforcement and investigations in foreign countries in the Americas, Africa, Europe, and Asia.

Although outdated and overcrowded, the J. Edgar Hoover FBI Building remains the headquarters of the FBI until a suitable replacement can be found.

Partners in Fighting Crime

FBI special agents may be called upon to assist other local, state, and federal law enforcement agencies. The FBI may also be called upon to work closely with international agencies like **Interpol** and law enforcement agencies in other countries around the world. These partnerships often take the form of joint task forces, in which several agencies work together to tackle a particular crime. These task forces target crimes such as terrorism, cyber crime, crimes against children, and gang-related crime. The agencies involved in these task forces pool their talents, knowledge, and skills into a single team with a shared goal.

It's not uncommon to see the FBI working alongside members of local law enforcement agencies, especially on cases involving terrorism or organized crime.

The FBI also partners with private agencies and organizations. The FBI teams with members of industrial, academic, religious, nonprofit, and community organizations to share information and build healthy relationships.

Internships with the FBI

The FBI offers both paid and unpaid internships to college students who might be interested in a career with the agency. Undergraduate and graduate students accepted to an internship usually work alongside FBI employees in one of the 56 field offices around the country. The FBI also has two specialized internships: the Cyber Internship Program and the Visiting Scientist Program. Cyber interns have the opportunity to assist in investigating and preventing cyber threats from around the world. The Visiting Scientist Program allows students to work at the FBI Laboratory at Quantico.

The FBI frequently conducts events around the country to recruit, or gather, new hires. To reach many possible employees, the FBI sends representatives to military career fairs, college job fairs, and job fairs for many other professional and student organizations.

Like other organizations, the FBI only wants the best of the best. Recruiting events and job fairs are the perfect place for the FBI to find future agents.

The FBI Today

The FBI must continue to grow and change to keep up with the criminals it chases. When the FBI was first created, most of the crimes it investigated involved bank robbers, gangsters, and kidnappers.

However, the FBI is no longer simply a law enforcement agency. As the 21st century began, the FBI grew into an agency focused on gathering and analyzing intelligence. Today, the men and women who work for the FBI face high-tech computer criminals and terrorists who may be hiding behind a computer or a false identity. In order to face these new threats, the FBI will need intelligent and committed men and women, especially those with a strong background in science and technology. Do you have what it takes to be an FBI special agent?

Glossary

analyze: To study something deeply.

applicant: Someone who applies for a job.

corruption: Illegal or dishonest behavior, especially by people in power.

forensics: The use of science and technology to investigate and establish facts in a court of law.

hostage: Someone who is being held against their will.

Interpol: An organization of over 190 national police forces that fights international crime.

jurisdiction: The range of judicial or law enforcement authority.

personnel: A group of people who work at a place.

Prohibition: A period of time from 1920 to 1933 in the United States when it was illegal to make or sell alcohol.

tactical: Relating to a plan or technique designed to reach a desired result.

task force: A group of experts formed to investigate or solve a specific problem.

terrorist: Someone who uses violence for political aims.

testify: To give a statement under oath, especially in court.

Index

Websites

Due to the changing nature of Internet links, PowerKids Press has developed an online list of websites related to the subject of this book. This site is updated regularly. Please use this link to access the list: www.powerkidslinks.com/fed/fbi